SHAWN MENDES
POP STAR

BY PEGGY CARAVANTES

Published by The Child's World®
1980 Lookout Drive • Mankato, MN 56003-1705
800-599-READ • www.childsworld.com

ISBN 9781503819979
LCCN 2016960921

Printed in the United States of America
PA02335

ABOUT THE AUTHOR

Peggy Caravantes is the award-winning author of over 25 nonfiction books
for young adults, middle grade, and children. A retired educator, she
lives in San Antonio, Texas, where she is an active community and church
volunteer. She enjoys research on any topic and likes to read mysteries in her
spare time.

TABLE OF
CONTENTS

FAST FACTS

Name

- Shawn Peter Raul Mendes

Birthdate

- August 8, 1998

Birthplace

- Toronto, Ontario, Canada

Fun Trivia

- Shawn played soccer and hockey before taking up music.
- Shawn's favorite foods are omelets, almonds, and chocolate chip cookies. He hates tomatoes.
- He works out at least once a day.
- Shawn tweets an average of four times a day.
- He speaks three languages: English, Spanish, and French.

Chapter 1

EARLY SUCCESS

Shawn Mendes was surprised. "Not in a million years did I think this would happen to me."[1] Overnight, Shawn had become a pop sensation. In August 2013, the Canadian teen posted another **cover** on YouTube. But posting covers of popular songs was not getting much response. Then one evening, he discovered Vine, a video-sharing app. No one seemed to be using it. Shawn decided to give it a try. Perched on a tall stool in his bedroom, he pulled his guitar close and began to sing. He covered a few notes of a Justin Bieber song, "As Long As You Love Me." He posted the six-second tune and went to bed. The next morning, he logged into his Vine account. He couldn't believe his eyes.

◀ **Shawn Mendes has performed in dozens of venues across the United States and Canada.**

There were 10,000 likes. Within a couple of weeks, he had 100,000 followers.

Only a month after that first Vine cover, he performed his **debut** concert in Toronto. A crowd of 600 tweens, mostly girls, pushed and shoved for a place in line. Once inside the auditorium, their high-pitched screams continued as they took endless photos with their phones. Some held pictures of Shawn, hoping to get his autograph after the concert. He appeared on stage, wearing khaki **chinos** and a gray sweatshirt. He yelled to the audience, "Y'all ready?" They screamed back, "Yeah!"[3] He began with the song "Give Me Love," by his **idol** Ed Sheeran.

Arms swaying, the girls joined Shawn in singing each of the concert's eight songs. They knew all the words.

▲ It didn't take long for people to gather to see Shawn sing.

At the end of the concert, he held a brief Q&A. Someone asked if he had a girlfriend. When he answered that he did not, the girls screamed loudly. This audience enthusiasm was just a preview of what he could expect in the future.

Chapter 2

RAPID CLIMB

S hawn sat in a red booth in an empty coffee house, waiting for words to come to his mind. He was wearing the usual plaid shirt with the sleeves rolled to his elbows. A waitress in a short red dress brought Shawn a mug filled with coffee. They didn't speak, and she went back to cleaning. As words formed in his mind, he felt as if he could see them everywhere. They were on the tables, the hanging lamps, and the counter. Clasping a pen, Shawn wrote them down. When he finished, he walked out of the coffee shop. This scene was the video for Shawn's first single, "Life of the Party." It was released in June 2014. At that time it ranked number 24 on Hot 100. Fifteen-year-old Shawn became the youngest person to debut in the top 25.

◀ Two months after Shawn released his first album, he was the opening act for singer Austin Mahone.

This was the beginning of his climb in the music world. A month later he released his debut **EP**, *Shawn Mendes*. It became #5 on Billboard 200. For the rest of 2014, Shawn toured the United States. He also released his second single, "Something Big," and won a Teen Choice Award. It wasn't just tweens who watched Shawn on social media. Agent Andrew Gertler also discovered Shawn that way. He offered Shawn a contract to sing under the Island Records label.

Before Shawn came on the music scene, he was an ordinary teenager. He lived with his parents and younger sister, Aaliyah. They lived in Pickering, a city near Toronto. He was a student at Pine Ridge Secondary School when he attended a leadership camp that touched his life. It taught him how to set goals and increased his **self-confidence**. Shawn thought everyone should attend the camp. But many students at Pine Ridge did not have the money to pay for it. So Shawn helped out.

◀ **Shawn won the Teen Choice Award for Choice Web Star in the Music category in 2015.**

He gave a special concert on January 18, 2015. It raised money so that all his classmates could attend.

In February 2015, he made his own world tour. Everywhere he went, he was met by screaming fans. Then in May, Taylor Swift asked him to open in the United States for her *1989* world tour. He freaked out when he received the invitation, but then accepted with a happy emoji. His typical set on the Swift tour included his singles "Life of the Party" and "Something Big." Between performances, Shawn wrote more of his own music.

"There's just so much happening. I would have exploded if I had to wait another year to show the world what I'm capable of."[4]

—*Mendes commenting about how rapidly his life changed.*

◄ **Shawn was born to perform.**

Chapter 3

THE FUTURE IS BRIGHT

Shawn loves to tell stories from every place he performs. On November 30, 2014, at his concert at the Danforth Music Hall in Toronto, Shawn strolled onto stage. He was holding the guitar he had learned to play less than two years earlier. Ready to sing, he looked out across a sea of 1,000 young girls—all screaming. In their hands they held brightly colored paper hearts. Surprised, Shawn asked them how they had planned the display. They answered with more screams. He asked for the house lights to be turned on. He wanted to see the girls' faces.

◄ **Before and after his events, Shawn often stops by the crowd of fans to take pictures.**

▲ Shawn's fans show their passion at the MuchMusic Video Awards in Toronto in 2015.

He wanted to show them how important they were to him. He wanted to see them as real people.

Shawn blushed as he described how, at another show, 300 eager fans surrounded his tour bus. When some girls broke through a fence, Shawn ran. In his dressing room, he could still hear their **muffled** screams.

Two hundred fans once gathered at the top of a hill to watch Shawn pose for publicity pictures.

While Shawn crouched low in a pose, a few daring girls sneaked down the hill. They broke through the yellow tape intended to hold them back. They marched toward Shawn slowly, pulling their feet from wet sand with each step. The director charged toward them and warned they would be barred from Shawn's concert that night. The girls hesitated for a few minutes. Then, because no one wanted to miss Shawn's show, they trudged back up the hill.

Shawn's success continued. His first full-length album, *Handwritten*, debuted #1 on Billboard 200 in early 2015. One of the album's singles, "Stitches," had 204 million streams and reached #4 on Billboard Hot 100 in April 2015. According to rhythm and blues singer JoJo, "He has his finger on the pulse of girls' hearts."[5]

It was September 2016, and Shawn was set to play for a sold-out crowd. Heart thumping, he walked out to the small stage in the middle of Madison Square Garden. He sat down at the keyboard. Before his fingers even touched the keys, the shouting began.

▲ Shawn performs for a huge crowd on the *Today* show on July 8, 2016.

The fans' noise was even louder than usual. Just his saying "hello" caused a **frenzy**. Shawn welcomed it. He told the crowd: "I cannot hear myself at all . . . I love that so much."[6] He then turned back to the keyboard and introduced his second album, *Illuminate*.

Having such devoted fans helped Shawn become more confident in his performances. However, Shawn recognizes that fame can be brief.

"My biggest fear is that one day, not as many people show up, or one day, not many people favorite a tweet."[7] In the meantime he has added another feature to his career. He signed with the Wilhelmina agency to become a model.

"When you have an opportunity like I had, it would have been absolutely crazy to not take advantage and at least try to make something of it."[8]

—Mendes describing his desire to make a career out of his social media success.

THINK ABOUT IT

- Social media quickly shot Shawn to fame. What do you think are some drawbacks to becoming an instant sensation?
- Shawn's first popularity was with tweens. Now that he is older, what changes do you think he will make to appeal to an older audience?
- Shawn speaks three languages. How do you think he can use this ability to further his career?

GLOSSARY

chinos (CHEE-noz): Chinos are pants made of a khaki material. On stage Shawn usually wears chinos and a plaid shirt.

cover (KUHV-ur): A cover is a new recording of a song previously recorded or made popular by another person. Shawn Mendes sang a cover of an Ed Sheeran song.

debut (day-BYOO): A debut is a first performance or appearance. Shawn made his singing debut on Vine.

EP: EP stands for extended play; it refers to a recording that has several tracks but not enough to qualify as an album. Shawn's first EP shot to #5 on Billboard 200.

frenzy (FREN-zee): A frenzy is a great and often wild activity. Shawn's fans were in a frenzy whenever he appeared.

idol (EYE-duhl): An idol is a greatly loved and admired person. Ed Sheeran was Shawn's idol because he both played and composed music.

muffled (MUHF-uhld): Muffled means to make a sound quieter. The dressing room walls muffled the screams of Shawn's fans.

self-confidence (SELF-KAHN-fi-duhns): Self-confidence is the belief a person has that he or she has the ability to succeed. Every concert brought Shawn more self-confidence.

SOURCE NOTES

1. Rob LeDonne. "Is 16-Year-Old Pop-Singer Shawn Mendes the Next Justin Bieber?" *Observer*. 16 January 2015. Web.

2. Ibid.

3. "Shawn Mendes Concert Experience." *YouTube*. 26 October 2013. Web.

4. Joe Coscarelli. "Shawn Mendes, Pop Idol, Is Not Banking on a Gimmick." *New York Times*. 20 September 2016. Web.

5. Rebecca Haithcoat. "Billboard Cover: Shawn Mendes Brings Back Hunky, Guitar-Strumming Sensitivity." *Billboard*. 25 August 2016. Web.

6. Elias Leight. "Pop Sensation Shawn Mendes on His New Album, *Illuminate*, Out Today." *Vogue*. 23 September 2016. Web.

7. Brittany Spanos. "Shawn Mendes: How a Toronto Teen Became the Superstar Next Door." *RollingStone*. 13 April 2016. Web.

8. Rob LeDonne. "Is 16-Year-Old Pop Singer Shawn Mendes the Next Justin Bieber?" *Observer*. 16 January 2015. Web.

TO LEARN MORE

Books

Bieber, Justin. *Justin Bieber: Just Getting Started*. New York, NY: HarperCollins, 2012.

Triumph Books. *Shawn Mendes: Superstar Next Door*. Chicago, IL: Triumph Books, 2016.

Zakarin, Debra Mostow. *Shawn Mendes: It's My Time*. New York, NY: Scholastic Inc., 2016.

Web Sites

Visit our Web site for links about Shawn Mendes:
childsworld.com/links

Note to Parents, Teachers, and Librarians: We routinely verify our Web links to make sure they are safe and active sites. So encourage your readers to check them out!

INDEX